AF413528

COLOR BY MATH PRACTICE BOOK FOR THE EXHAUSTED LEARNER

EASY MATH BOOK FOR KIDS

CHILDREN'S ARITHMETIC BOOKS

Speedy Publishing LLC

40 E. Main St. #1156

Newark, DE 19711

www.speedypublishing.com

Copyright 2018

All Rights reserved. No part of this book may be reproduced or used in any way or form or by any means whether electronic or mechanical, this means that you cannot record or photocopy any material ideas or tips that are provided in this book.

GET BUSY BUILDING YOUR MATH SKILLS WITH FUN COLOR BY MATH PAGES!

LET'S GET STARTED!

1   **2**   **3**   **4**   **5**   **6**

Solve then color all the answer using the color key.

This is a Bleed Through Page If You Are Using a Coloring Marker or Pen!

Find Other Great Titles By searching for Baby Professor on Your Favorite Book Retailer

Amazon.Com | Barnes & Noble (BN.Com) | Books A Million (BAM.Com)

BABY PROFESSOR

EDUCATION KIDS

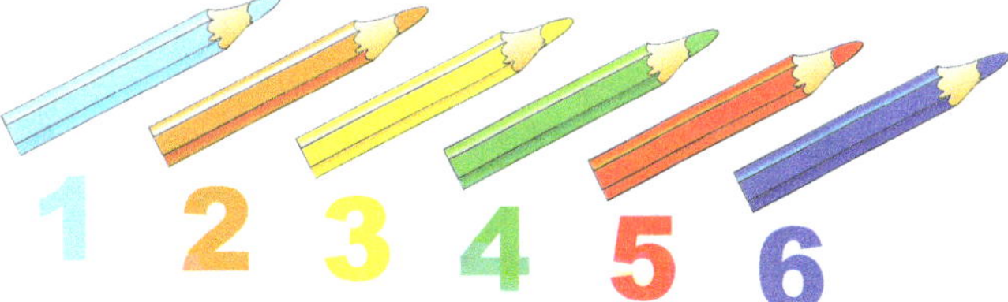

Solve then color all the answer using the color key.

This is a Bleed Through Page If You Are Using a Coloring Marker or Pen!
Find Other Great Titles By searching for Baby Professor on Your Favorite Book Retailer
Amazon.Com | Barnes & Noble (BN.Com) | Books A Million (BAM.Com)

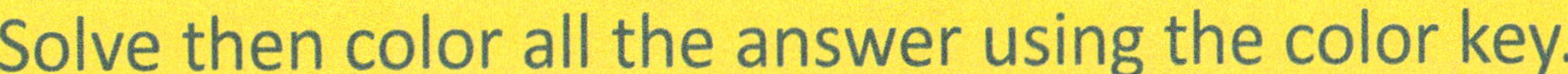

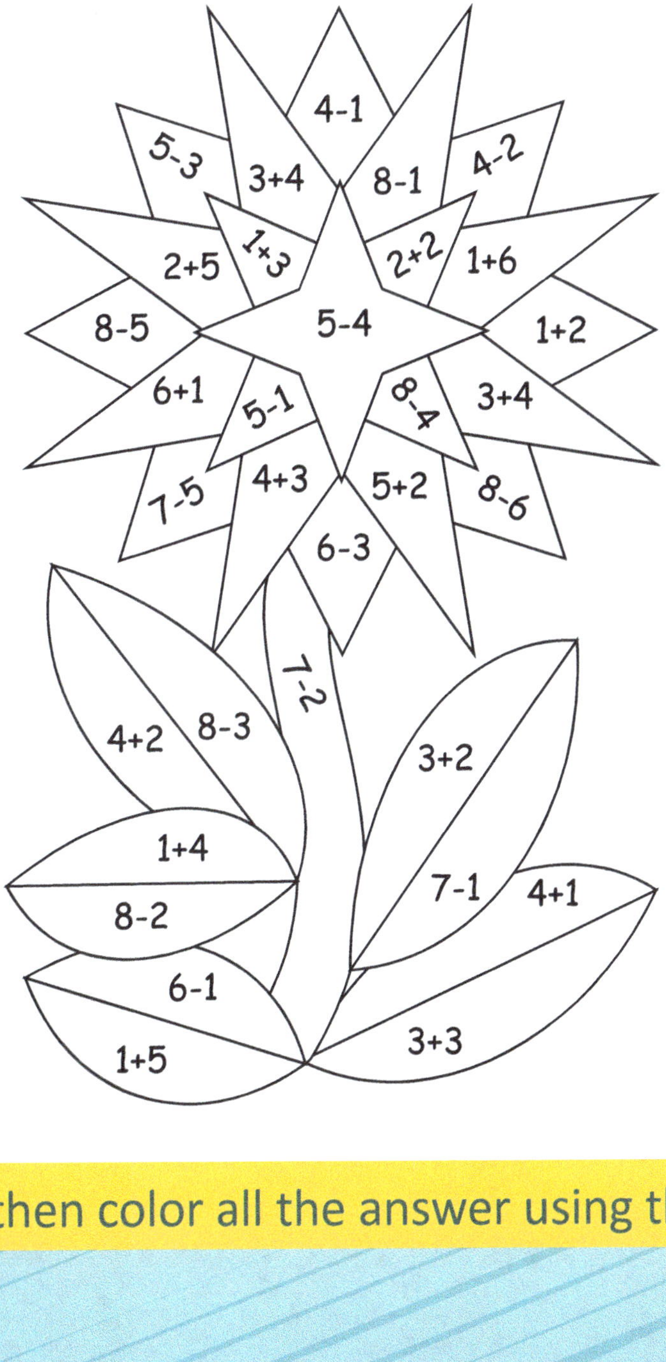

1
2
3
4
5
6
7

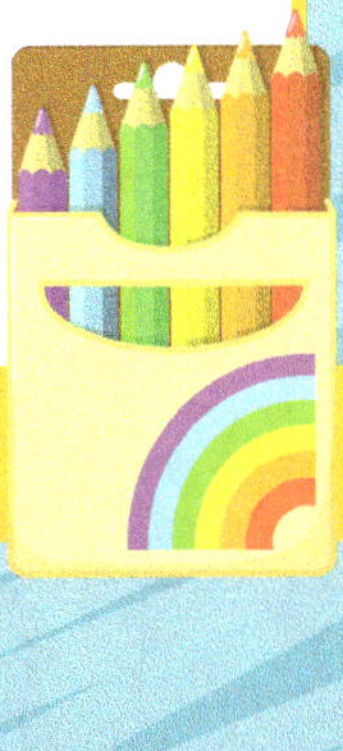

Solve then color all the answer using the color key.

This is a Bleed Through Page If You Are Using a Coloring Marker or Pen!
Find Other Great Titles By searching for Baby Professor on Your Favorite Book Retailer
Amazon.Com | Barnes & Noble (BN.Com) | Books A Million (BAM.Com)

BABY PROFESSOR
EDUCATION KIDS

Solve then color all the answer using the color key.

This is a Bleed Through Page If You Are Using a Coloring Marker or Pen!
Find Other Great Titles By searching for Baby Professor on Your Favorite Book Retailer
Amazon.Com | Barnes & Noble (BN.Com) | Books A Million (BAM.Com)

BABY PROFESSOR
EDUCATION KIDS

Solve then color all the answer using the color key.

This is a Bleed Through Page If You Are Using a Coloring Marker or Pen!

Find Other Great Titles By searching for Baby Professor on Your Favorite Book Retailer

Amazon.Com | Barnes & Noble (BN.Com) | Books A Million (BAM.Com)

BABY PROFESSOR
EDUCATION KIDS

Solve then color all the answer using the color key.

This is a Bleed Through Page If You Are Using a Coloring Marker or Pen!
Find Other Great Titles By searching for Baby Professor on Your Favorite Book Retailer
Amazon.Com | Barnes & Noble (BN.Com) | Books A Million (BAM.Com)

BABY PROFESSOR
EDUCATION KIDS

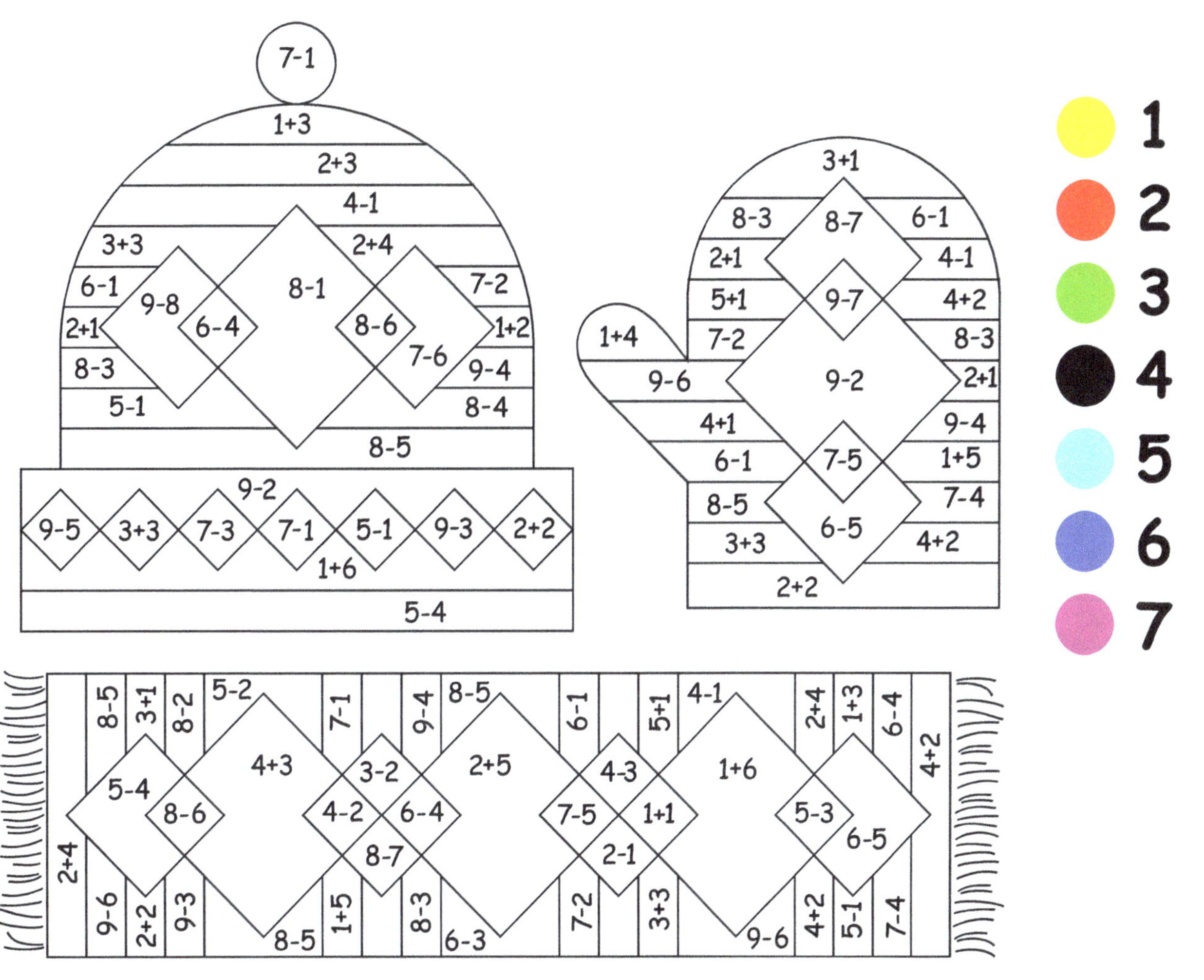

Solve then color all the answer using the color key.

This is a Bleed Through Page If You Are Using a Coloring Marker or Pen!
Find Other Great Titles By searching for Baby Professor on Your Favorite Book Retailer
Amazon.Com | Barnes & Noble (BN.Com) | Books A Million (BAM.Com)

BABY PROFESSOR
EDUCATION KIDS

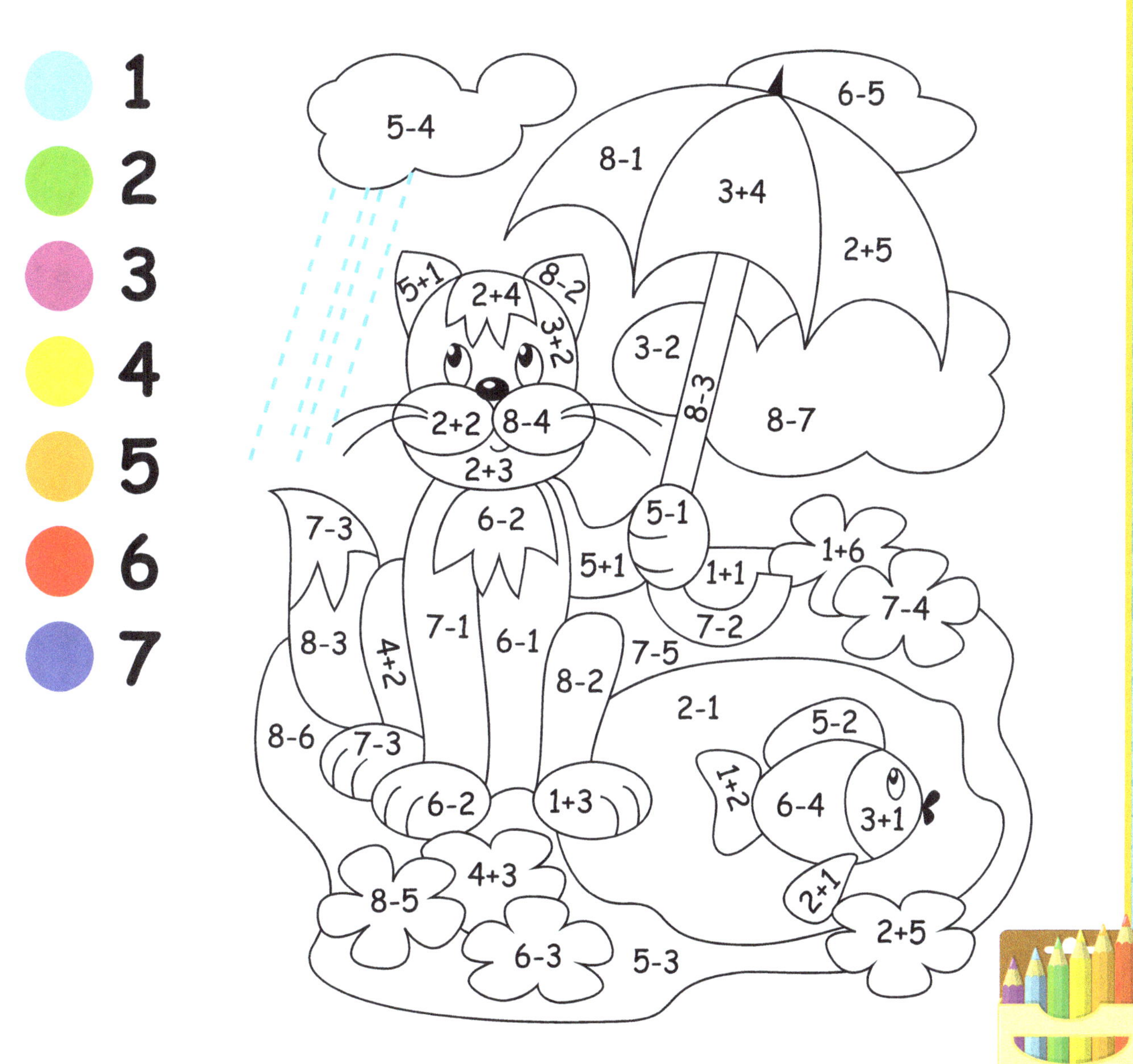

Solve then color all the answer using the color key.

This is a Bleed Through Page If You Are Using a Coloring Marker or Pen!
Find Other Great Titles By searching for Baby Professor on Your Favorite Book Retailer
Amazon.Com | Barnes & Noble (BN.Com) | Books A Million (BAM.Com)

Solve then color all the answer using the color key.

This is a Bleed Through Page If You Are Using a Coloring Marker or Pen!
Find Other Great Titles By searching for Baby Professor on Your Favorite Book Retailer
Amazon.Com | Barnes & Noble (BN.Com) | Books A Million (BAM.Com)

5-3 =

2+3 =

3+6 =

8-4 =

7+1 =

3-0 =

4+3 =

9-3 =

Solve then color all the answer using the color key.

This is a Bleed Through Page If You Are Using a Coloring Marker or Pen!
Find Other Great Titles By searching for Baby Professor on Your Favorite Book Retailer
Amazon.Com | Barnes & Noble (BN.Com) | Books A Million (BAM.Com)

BABY PROFESSOR
EDUCATION KIDS

2+2 =

4+2 =

7+1 =

9-7 =

2+3 =

6-3 =

2+5 =

5+4 =

Solve then color all the answer using the color key.

This is a Bleed Through Page If You Are Using a Coloring Marker or Pen!
Find Other Great Titles By searching for Baby Professor on Your Favorite Book Retailer
Amazon.Com | Barnes & Noble (BN.Com) | Books A Million (BAM.Com)

BABY PROFESSOR
EDUCATION KIDS

5+3 =

10-1 =

8-6 =

4+3 =

2+1 =

1+5 =

2+2 =

9-4 =

Solve then color all the answer using the color key.

This is a Bleed Through Page If You Are Using a Coloring Marker or Pen!
Find Other Great Titles By searching for Baby Professor on Your Favorite Book Retailer
Amazon.Com | Barnes & Noble (BN.Com) | Books A Million (BAM.Com)

BABY PROFESSOR
EDUCATION KIDS

2+1 =

4-2 =

1+3 =

5-4 =

1+4 =

3+3 =

3+4 =

10-2 =

Solve then color all the answer using the color key.

This is a Bleed Through Page If You Are Using a Coloring Marker or Pen!

Find Other Great Titles By searching for Baby Professor on Your Favorite Book Retailer

Amazon.Com | Barnes & Noble (BN.Com) | Books A Million (BAM.Com)

BABY PROFESSOR

EDUCATION KIDS

Color key:

1 =
2 =
3 =
4 =
5 =
6 =
7 =
8 =

Equations in the picture:

3 1+2 1+8 2+1 4-1

5+4 7+2 6+3

2+7

3+6 1+5 2+4 5+1 2+2 2 4+5

4+2 7-1 4+1 2+3 6-1 1+1

3+3 2+4 1+5 2-1 6 2+1

8+1 3+2 3+2 3-2 5+4 4-2 6

7-2 5-3 3+1 5-2 1+8

1+4 1+3 7 2+2 1+2

7+1 3+4 2+2

2+6 8-1 5-1 3 1+1 2+6

6+2 4+3 1+7

Solve then color all the answer using the color key.

This is a Bleed Through Page If You Are Using a Coloring Marker or Pen!
Find Other Great Titles By searching for Baby Professor on Your Favorite Book Retailer
Amazon.Com | Barnes & Noble (BN.Com) | Books A Million (BAM.Com)

BABY PROFESSOR
EDUCATION KIDS

2 =

3 =

4 =

5 =

6 =

7 =

8 =

9 =

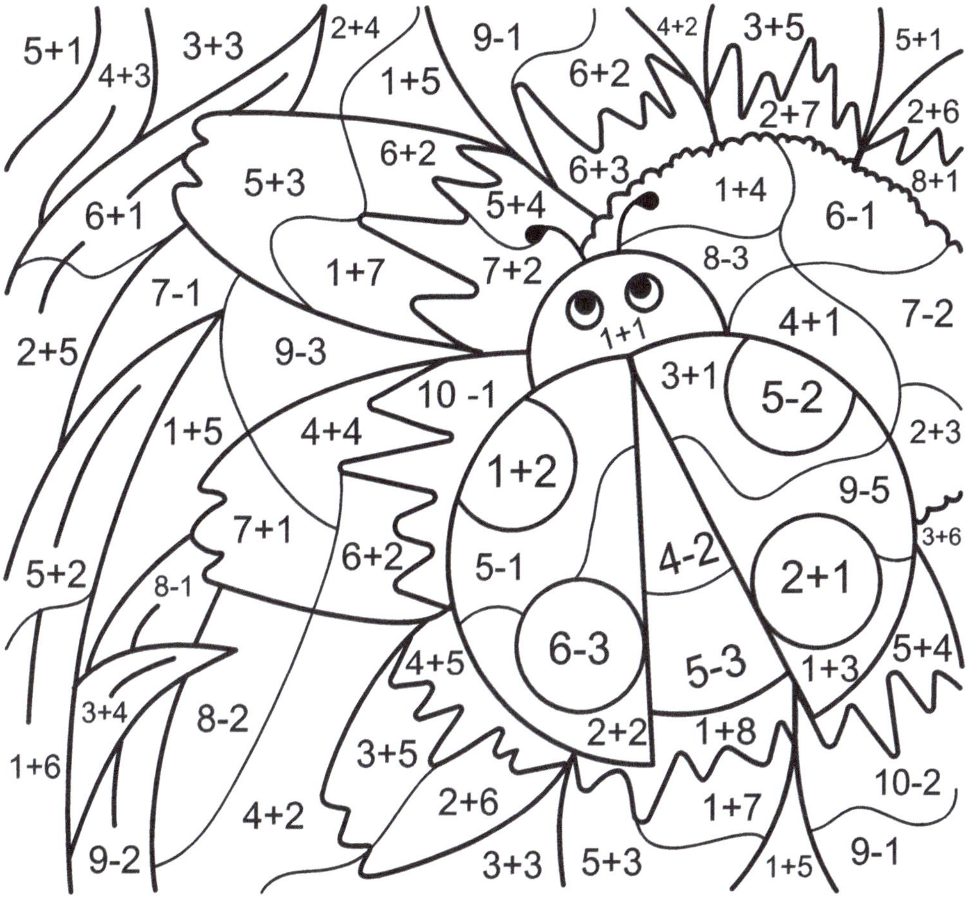

5+1   4+3   3+3   2+4   9-1   4+2   3+5   5+1
                          1+5   6+2   2+7   2+6
6+1   5+3   6+2   6+3   1+4   6-1   8+1
              5+4
7-1   1+7   7+2   8-3
2+5   9-3   1+1   4+1   7-2
        1+5   4+4   10 -1   3+1   5-2   2+3
5+2   7+1   1+2   9-5   3+6
    8-1   6+2   5-1   4-2   2+1
        4+5   6-3   5-3   1+3   5+4
3+4   8-2   2+2   1+8   10-2
1+6   3+5   2+6   1+7
    9-2   4+2   3+3   5+3   1+5   9-1

This is a Bleed Through Page If You Are Using a Coloring Marker or Pen!
Find Other Great Titles By searching for Baby Professor on Your Favorite Book Retailer
Amazon.Com | Barnes & Noble (BN.Com) | Books A Million (BAM.Com)

BABY PROFESSOR
EDUCATION KIDS

1 =	(black)
2 =	(yellow)
3 =	(light yellow)
4 =	(orange)
5 =	(light blue)
6 =	(purple/blue)
7 =	(white)
8 =	(lavender)

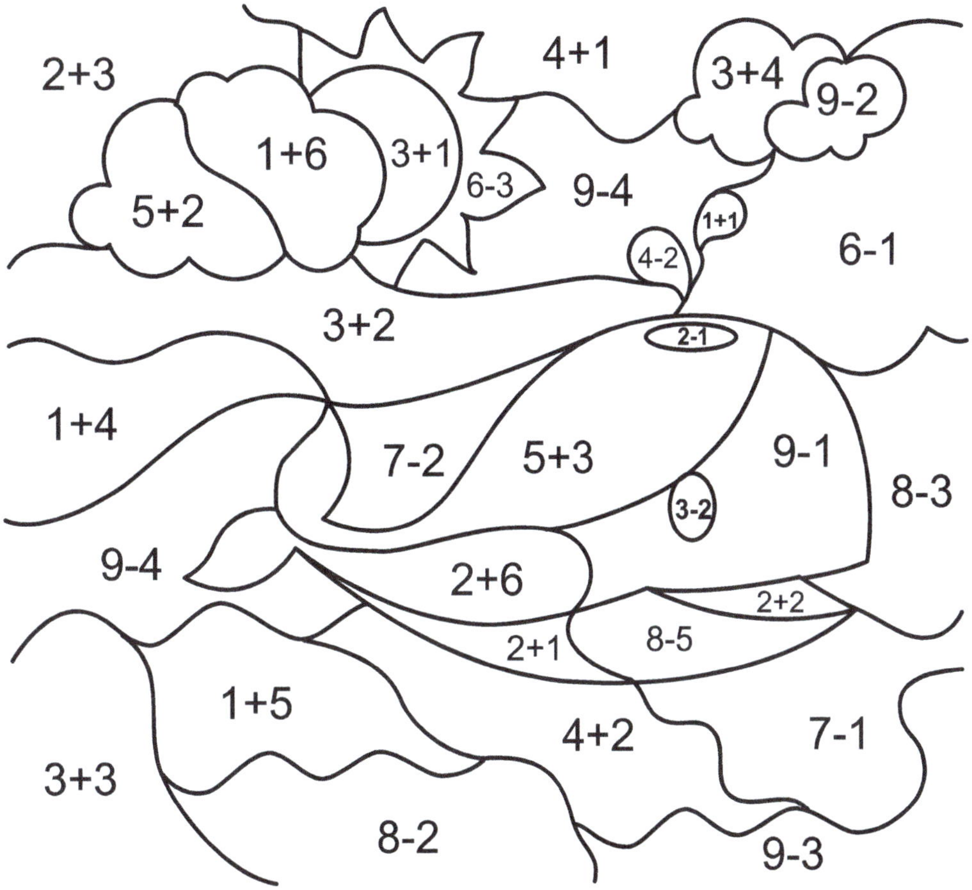

2+3

4+1

3+4   9-2

1+6   3+1

5+2   6-3   9-4

1+1

4-2   6-1

3+2

2-1

1+4

7-2   5+3   9-1   8-3

3-2

9-4   2+6

2+2

2+1   8-5

1+5   4+2   7-1

3+3

8-2   9-3

LET'S TRY MULTIPLICATION!

MULTIPLICATION TABLE

1

1 × 1 = 1
1 × 2 = 2
1 × 3 = 3
1 × 4 = 4
1 × 5 = 5
1 × 6 = 6
1 × 7 = 7
1 × 8 = 8
1 × 9 = 9
1 × 10 = 10

2

2 × 1 = 2
2 × 2 = 4
2 × 3 = 6
2 × 4 = 8
2 × 5 = 10
2 × 6 = 12
2 × 7 = 14
2 × 8 = 16
2 × 9 = 18
2 × 10 = 20

3

3 × 1 = 3
3 × 2 = 6
3 × 3 = 9
3 × 4 = 12
3 × 5 = 15
3 × 6 = 18
3 × 7 = 21
3 × 8 = 24
3 × 9 = 27
3 × 10 = 30

4

4 × 1 = 4
4 × 2 = 8
4 × 3 = 12
4 × 4 = 16
4 × 5 = 20
4 × 6 = 24
4 × 7 = 28
4 × 8 = 32
4 × 9 = 36
4 × 10 = 40

5

5 × 1 = 5
5 × 2 = 10
5 × 3 = 15
5 × 4 = 20
5 × 5 = 25
5 × 6 = 30
5 × 7 = 35
5 × 8 = 40
5 × 9 = 45
5 × 10 = 50

6

6 × 1 = 6
6 × 2 = 12
6 × 3 = 18
6 × 4 = 24
6 × 5 = 30
6 × 6 = 36
6 × 7 = 42
6 × 8 = 48
6 × 9 = 54
6 × 10 = 60

7

7 × 1 = 7
7 × 2 = 14
7 × 3 = 21
7 × 4 = 28
7 × 5 = 35
7 × 6 = 42
7 × 7 = 49
7 × 8 = 56
7 × 9 = 63
7 × 10 = 70

8

8 × 1 = 8
8 × 2 = 16
8 × 3 = 24
8 × 4 = 32
8 × 5 = 40
8 × 6 = 48
8 × 7 = 56
8 × 8 = 64
8 × 9 = 72
8 × 10 = 80

9

9 × 1 = 9
9 × 2 = 18
9 × 3 = 27
9 × 4 = 36
9 × 5 = 45
9 × 6 = 54
9 × 7 = 63
9 × 8 = 72
9 × 9 = 81
9 × 10 = 90

10

10 × 1 = 10
10 × 2 = 20
10 × 3 = 30
10 × 4 = 40
10 × 5 = 50
10 × 6 = 60
10 × 7 = 70
10 × 8 = 80
10 × 9 = 90
10 × 10 = 100

Solve then color all the answer using the color key.

8 12 16 20 24 28 32 36 40

This is a Bleed Through Page If You Are Using a Coloring Marker or Pen!
Find Other Great Titles By searching for Baby Professor on Your Favorite Book Retailer
Amazon.Com | Barnes & Noble (BN.Com) | Books A Million (BAM.Com)

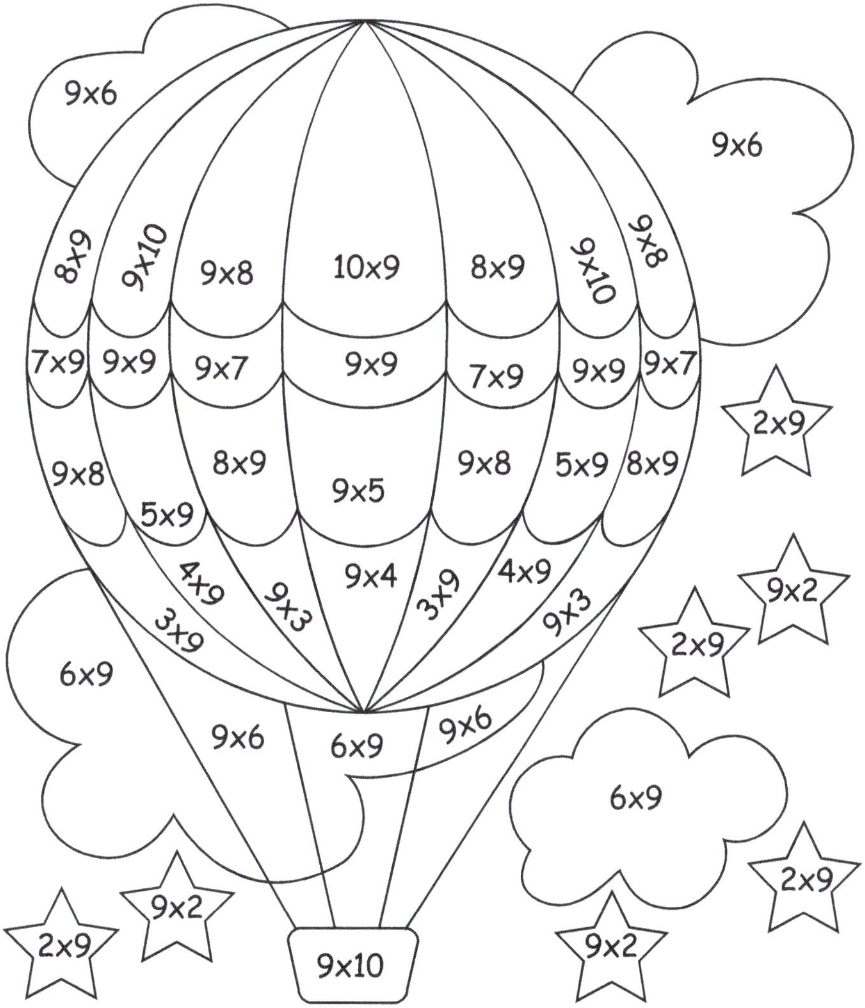

18 27 36 45 54 63 72 81 90

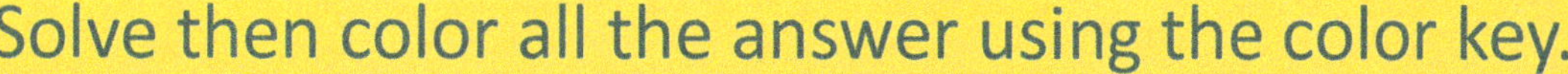

Solve then color all the answer using the color key.

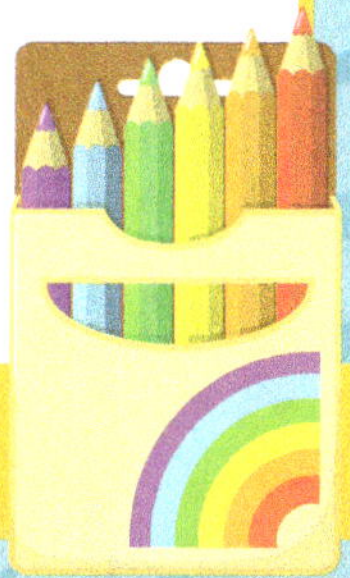

This is a Bleed Through Page If You Are Using a Coloring Marker or Pen!
Find Other Great Titles By searching for Baby Professor on Your Favorite Book Retailer
Amazon.Com | Barnes & Noble (BN.Com) | Books A Million (BAM.Com)

10

15

20

25

30

35

40

45

50

Solve then color all the answer using the color key.

This is a Bleed Through Page If You Are Using a Coloring Marker or Pen!
Find Other Great Titles By searching for Baby Professor on Your Favorite Book Retailer
Amazon.Com | Barnes & Noble (BN.Com) | Books A Million (BAM.Com)

BABY PROFESSOR
EDUCATION KIDS

3x7
3x8
3x7
3x6
3x7
3x7
3x5
3x9
3x10
3x8
3x2
3x3
2x3
3x3
3x2
3x3
2x3
3x4
3x6
3x6
3x4
3x9
3x9
3x4
3x3
3x3
3x5
3x6
3x6
3x5
3x5
3x5
3x5
3x3
3x3
2x3
3x7
3x10
3x7
3x6
3x8
3x7
3x3
3x2
3x3
2x3
3x3
3x2
3x6
3x6
3x8
3x10
3x8
3x3
3x3
6 9 12 15 18 21 24 27 30

Solve then color all the answer using the color key.

This is a Bleed Through Page If You Are Using a Coloring Marker or Pen!

Find Other Great Titles By searching for Baby Professor on Your Favorite Book Retailer

Amazon.Com | Barnes & Noble (BN.Com) | Books A Million (BAM.Com)

Solve then color all the answer using the color key.

This is a Bleed Through Page If You Are Using a Coloring Marker or Pen!
Find Other Great Titles By searching for *Baby Professor* on Your Favorite Book Retailer
Amazon.Com | Barnes & Noble (BN.Com) | Books A Million (BAM.Com)

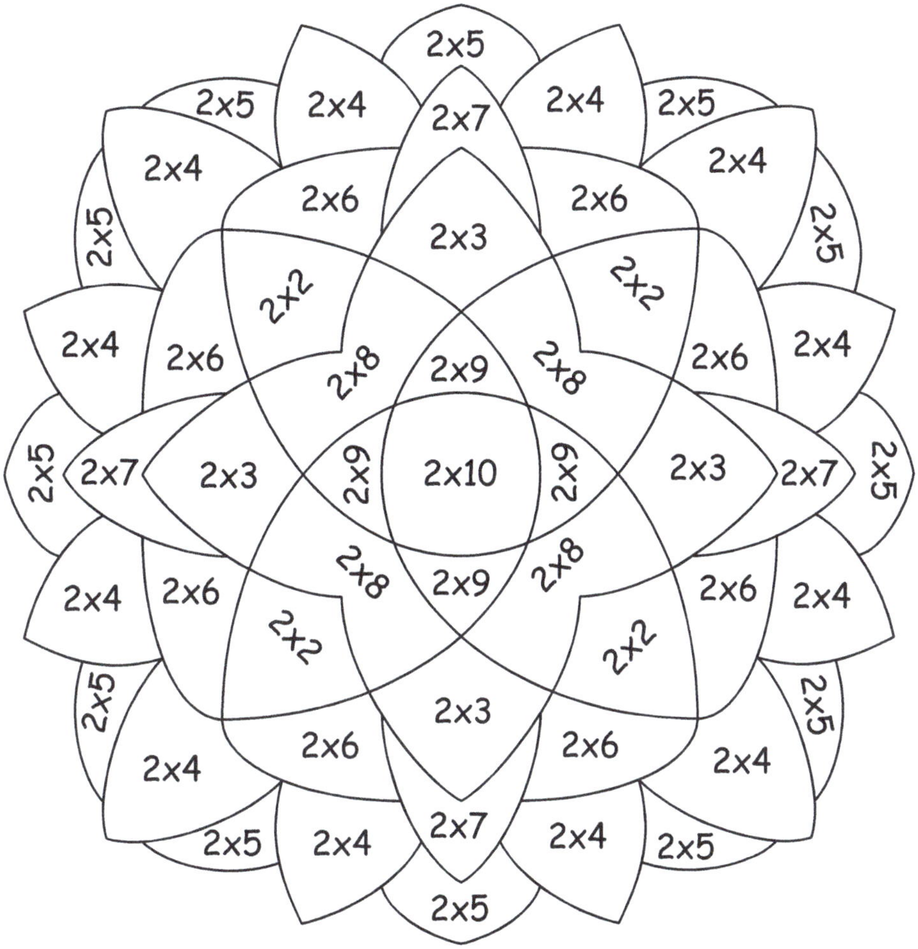

4 6 8 10 12 14 16 18 20

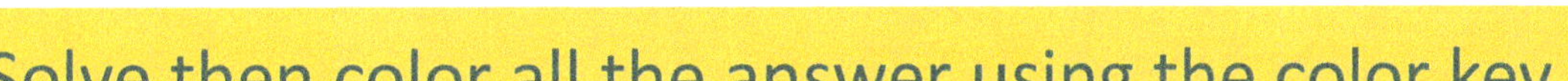

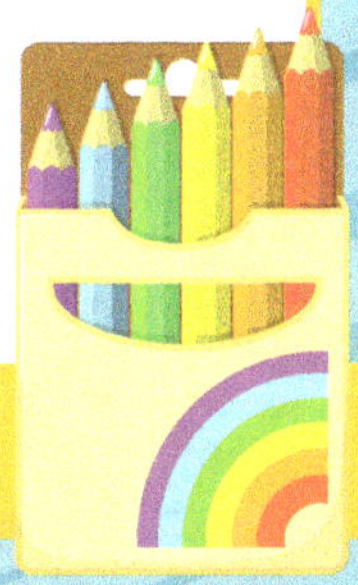

Solve then color all the answer using the color key.

This is a Bleed Through Page If You Are Using a Coloring Marker or Pen!
Find Other Great Titles By searching for Baby Professor on Your Favorite Book Retailer
Amazon.Com | Barnes & Noble (BN.Com) | Books A Million (BAM.Com)

BABY PROFESSOR
EDUCATION KIDS

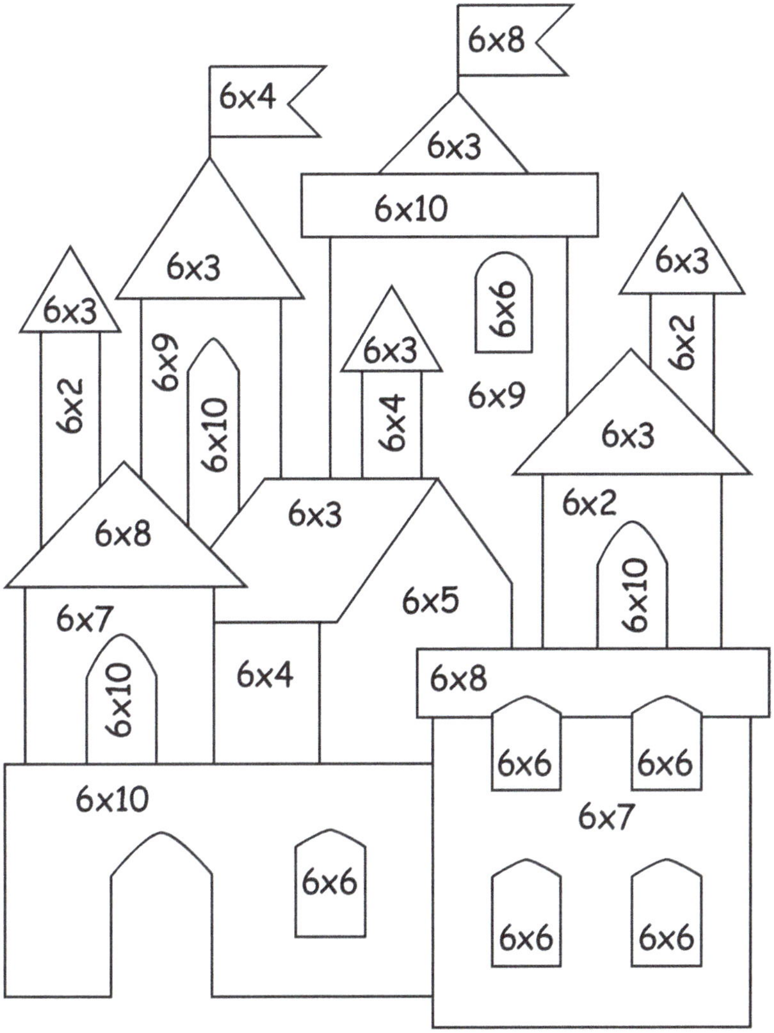

12	18	24	30	36	42	48	54	60

Solve then color all the answer using the color key.

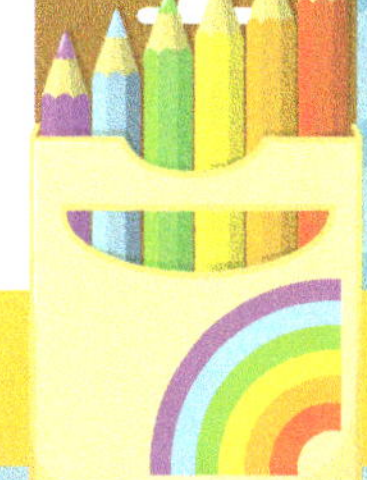

This is a Bleed Through Page If You Are Using a Coloring Marker or Pen!
Find Other Great Titles By searching for Baby Professor on Your Favorite Book Retailer
Amazon.Com | Barnes & Noble (BN.Com) | Books A Million (BAM.Com)

BABY PROFESSOR
EDUCATION KIDS

12
18
24
30
36
42
48
54
60

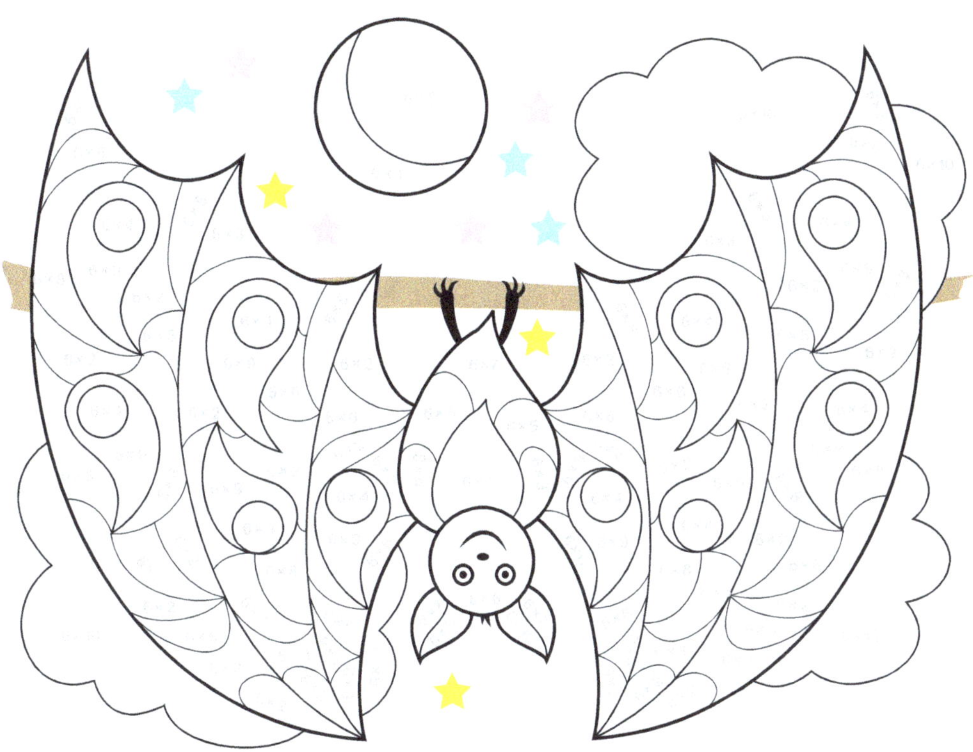

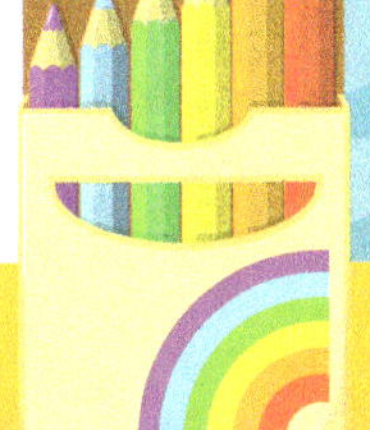

Solve then color all the answer using the color key.

This is a Bleed Through Page If You Are Using a Coloring Marker or Pen!
Find Other Great Titles By searching for Baby Professor on Your Favorite Book Retailer
Amazon.Com | Barnes & Noble (BN.Com) | Books A Million (BAM.Com)

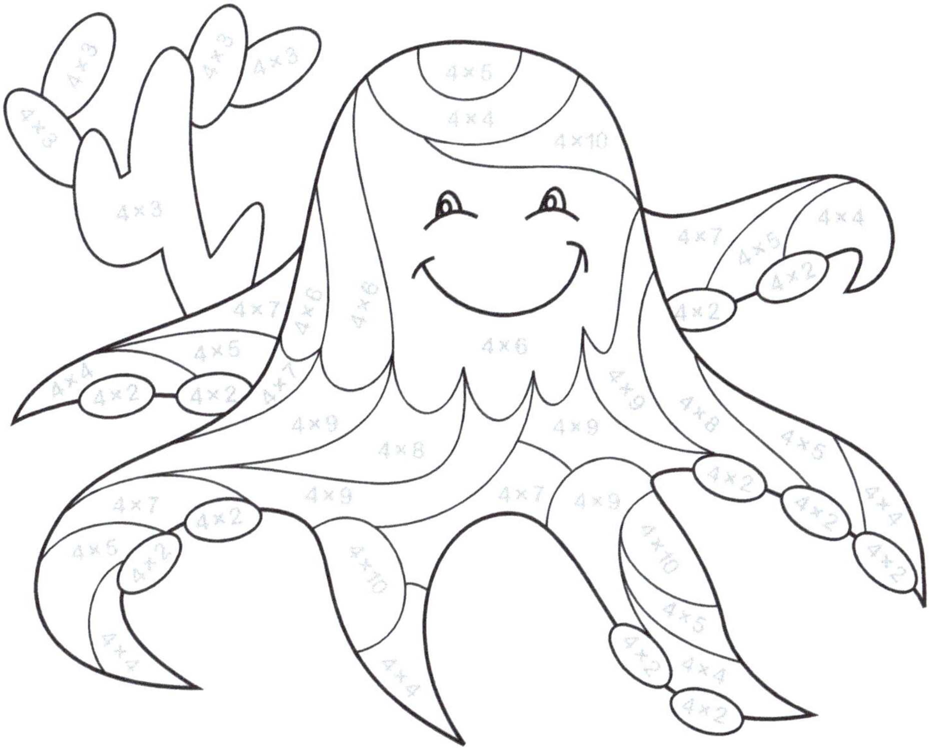

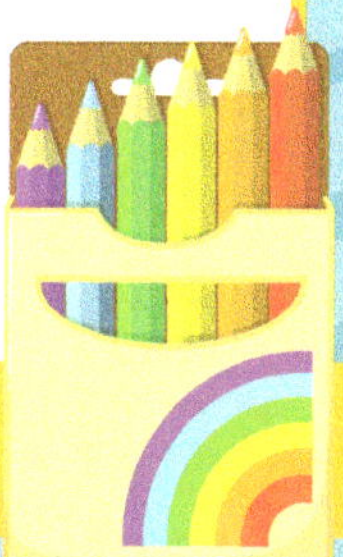

Solve then color all the answer using the color key.

This is a Bleed Through Page If You Are Using a Coloring Marker or Pen!
Find Other Great Titles By searching for *Baby Professor* on Your Favorite Book Retailer
Amazon.Com | Barnes & Noble (BN.Com) | Books A Million (BAM.Com)

BABY PROFESSOR
EDUCATION KIDS

4

6

8

10

12

14

16

18

20

Solve then color all the answer using the color key.

This is a Bleed Through Page If You Are Using a Coloring Marker or Pen!
Find Other Great Titles By searching for Baby Professor on Your Favorite Book Retailer
Amazon.Com | Barnes & Noble (BN.Com) | Books A Million (BAM.Com)

BABY PROFESSOR
EDUCATION KIDS

14
21
28
35
42
49
56
63
70

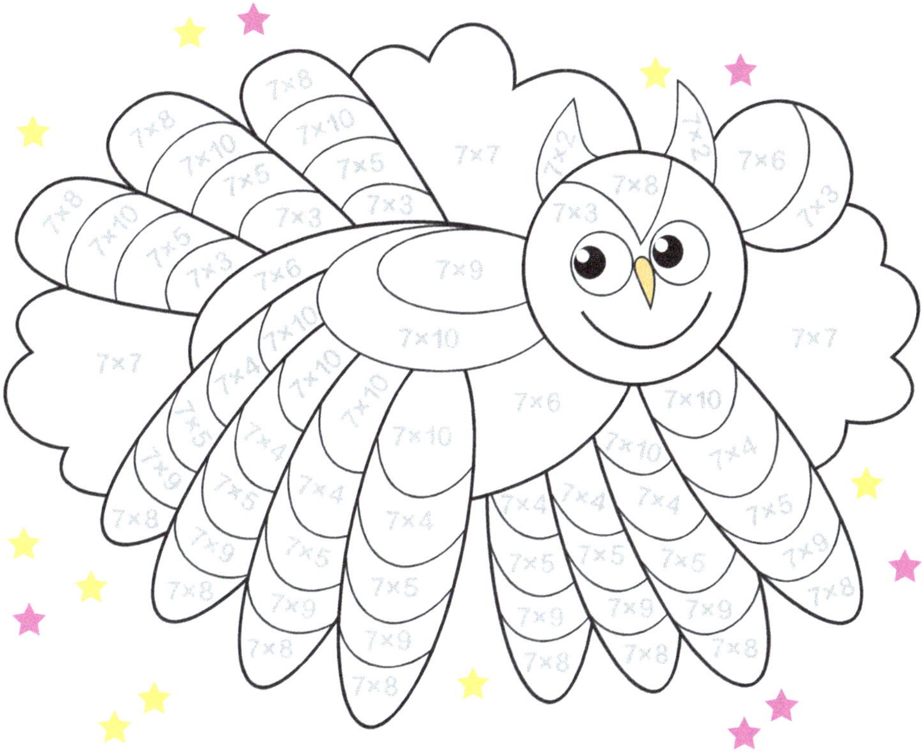

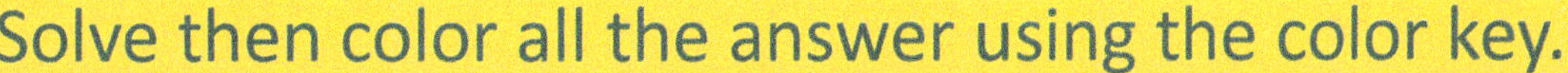

Solve then color all the answer using the color key.

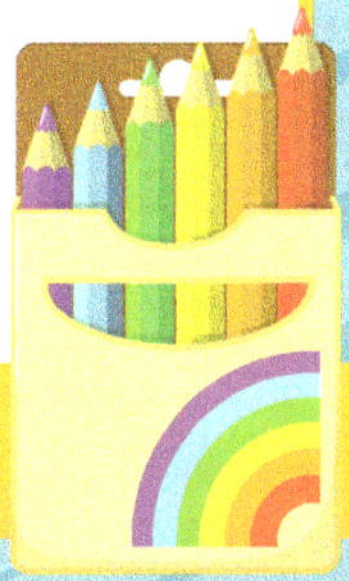

This is a Bleed Through Page If You Are Using a Coloring Marker or Pen!
Find Other Great Titles By searching for Baby Professor *on Your Favorite Book Retailer*
Amazon.Com | Barnes & Noble (BN.Com) | Books A Million (BAM.Com)

BABY PROFESSOR
EDUCATION KIDS

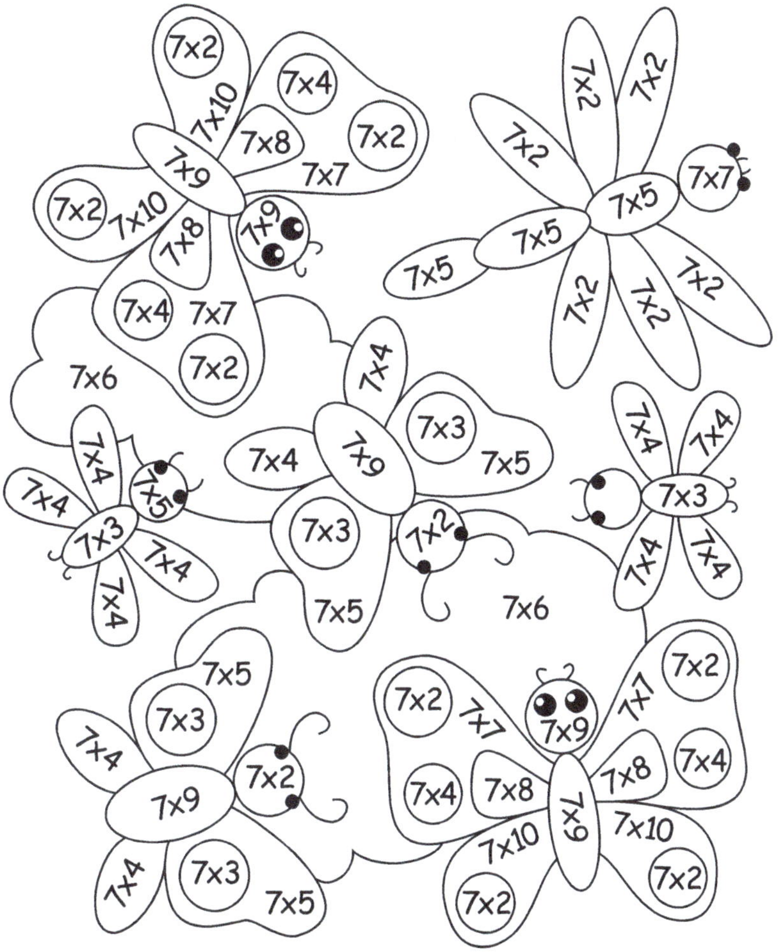

Solve then color all the answer using the color key.
14 21 28 35 42 49 56 63 70

This is a Bleed Through Page If You Are Using a Coloring Marker or Pen!
Find Other Great Titles By searching for Baby Professor on Your Favorite Book Retailer
Amazon.Com | Barnes & Noble (BN.Com) | Books A Million (BAM.Com)

BABY PROFESSOR
EDUCATION KIDS

Solve then color all the answer using the color key.

Visit

www.BabyProfessorBooks.com

to download Free Baby Professor eBooks
and view our catalog of new and exciting
Children's Books

www.ingramcontent.com/pod-product-compliance
Lightning Source LLC
Chambersburg PA
CBHW081353150726
48196CB00005BA/481